DIG IN!

12 EASY GARDENING PROJECTS USING KITCHEN SCRAPS

Kari Cornell

Photographs by

Jennifer S. Larson

Text copyright © 2018 by Kari Cornell
Photographs copyright © 2018 by Jennifer S. Larson

Millbrook Press
A division of Lerner Publishing Group, Inc.
241 First Avenue North
Minneapolis, MN 55401 USA

For reading levels and more information, look up this title at www.lernerbooks.com.

Main body text set in Frutiger LT Pro 10/13.
Typeface provided by Linotype AG.

Additional images in this book are used with the permission of: Only background/Shutterstock.com (paper background); USDA Plant Hardiness Zone Map, 2012. Agricultural Research Service, U.S. Department of Agriculture. Accessed from http://planthardiness.ars.usda.gov, p. 6; rixipix/Deposit Photos, p. 19; iStock.com/pederk, p. 24; iStock.com/SomchaiChoosiri, p. 31; iStock.com/wyoosumran, p. 36; iStock.com/Anastasia Stoeckmann, p. 39; iStock.com/margouillatphotos, p. 43; iStock.com/Terryfic3D, p. 52. Illustrations © Laura Westlund/Independent Picture Service.

Library of Congress Cataloging-in-Publication Data

Names: Cornell, Kari A., author.
Title: Dig in! : 12 easy gardening projects using kitchen scraps / by Kari Cornell.
Other titles: Twelve easy gardening projects using kitchen scraps
Description: Minneapolis, MN : Millbrook Press, [2018] | Includes index.
Identifiers: LCCN 2017010731 (print) | LCCN 2017013057 (ebook) | ISBN 9781512498646 (eb pdf) | ISBN 9781512430653 (lb : alk. paper)
Subjects: LCSH: Gardening—Juvenile literature. | Kitchen gardens—Juvenile literature.
Classification: LCC SB457 (ebook) | LCC SB457 .C658 2018 (print) | DDC 635—dc23

LC record available at https://lccn.loc.gov/2017010731

Manufactured in the United States of America
1-41656-23514-9/29/2017

TABLE OF CONTENTS

Introduction

Have you ever wished you could grow your own food from just a piece of something? Maybe a whole pizza from the very last slice? Growing pizza might sound like science fiction, but many foods already have this seemingly magic ability to regenerate.

Take garlic, for example, a common ingredient in pizza. By planting one single garlic clove, you can grow a whole new bulb of garlic, made up of many cloves.

How about putting some pepper slices on that pizza? By slicing open a pepper and planting a few of the seeds inside, you could grow a pepper plant that produces more peppers. Need a little spice for the sauce? Basil is an herb that is often used to flavor pizza. If you stick a branch from a basil plant in a jar of water, it will grow roots and become a new plant. And how about a salad with your meal? Did you know that romaine lettuce can be regrown by cutting off the root end and sticking it in a bowl of water? It's true!

Maybe "growing" a pizza isn't so far-fetched after all. In this book, you'll find instructions for growing garlic, peppers, basil, romaine lettuce, and many other fruits and vegetables—all from scraps, plants, and seeds that you harvest yourself. Ready? Set. Grow!

What Do Plants Need to Grow?

All plants need the right amount of sunlight, water, and healthy soil to grow strong and healthy. Sunlight and water are easy to provide. Plants that produce food usually need at least six hours of sunlight each day. Spend a day checking on the window or patch of soil where you plan to plant to see if the area gets enough sunlight. Check the site at 10:00 a.m., noon, 2:00 p.m., and 4:00 p.m., noting if the site is in sun or shade at those times. If the site does not get six hours of sun, look for another place to grow your garden.

Once the seeds or cuttings are planted, you'll need to check them each day to see if they need water. Stick your finger into the soil down to your first knuckle. If the soil is dry or the plants appear to be wilting, it's time to get out the watering can.

You can grow some herbs from cuttings (*left*). And lettuce will sprout from the root stem of another head of lettuce (*right*).

New seedlings will need a little water every day. Mature plants can go a bit longer. Most outside plants will need water at least every other day. Inside plants need to be watered one to two times per week.

Exactly what is healthy soil? Soil is made up of three parts: sand, silt, and clay. Each part has a different job to do. Sand pieces are the largest, allowing water to drain easily down to plant roots. The smallest pieces are clay, which hold moisture, allowing soil to stay damp after watering. Silt pieces are between the size of clay and sand particles. The ideal mixture of soil has equal parts sand, silt, and clay. In addition, it has a healthy dose of humus. Humus is organic matter made up of decaying leaves and plants. The potting soil you buy from the store is made up of the perfect mix of sand, silt, clay, and humus.

What Is pH?

Another piece of the healthy soil puzzle is the soil's pH. The pH is a chemical measurement. It affects how well plants are able to absorb nutrients. Certain plants, such as blueberries and strawberries, do well in soil that is acidic—a pH level of 4.0 to 6.5. Other plants, such as garlic and sunflowers, thrive in alkaline soil. Alkaline soil has a pH between 7.0 and 7.5. Many vegetables, such as pumpkins, peppers, celery, carrots, tomatoes, and lettuce like soil that is neutral—a pH of 6.0 to 7.0. Before transplanting seedlings into garden soil, always test the soil's pH. Soil testing kits can be found at your local garden or hardware store.

FIND YOUR ZONE!

There are many different growing zones in the United States. Different hardiness zones have different growing conditions, such as how much rain falls a year and how warm or cold it gets. These growing conditions are called climate. Look at the zone map below and find the zone in which you live. When planting your garden and the projects in this book, look up the last and first frost day in your zone. Then plant outside during the growing season between those dates. Your plants will likely die unless you bring them inside during the colder months. Paying attention to your zone will make your first gardening attempts easier.

PLANT HARDINESS ZONE MAP

Average Annual Extreme Low Temperature 1976-2005

Temp (F)	Zone	Temp (C)
-60 to -55	1a	-51.1 to -48.3
-55 to -50	1b	-48.3 to -45.6
-50 to -45	2a	-45.6 to -42.8
-45 to -40	2b	-42.8 to -40
-40 to -35	3a	-40 to -37.2
-35 to -30	3b	-37.2 to -34.4
-30 to -25	4a	-34.4 to -31.7
-25 to -20	4b	-31.7 to -28.9
-20 to -15	5a	-28.9 to -26.1
-15 to -10	5b	-26.1 to -23.3
-10 to -5	6a	-23.3 to -20.6
-5 to 0	6b	-20.6 to -17.8
0 to 5	7a	-17.8 to -15
5 to 10	7b	-15 to -12.2
10 to 15	8a	-12.2 to -9.4
15 to 20	8b	-9.4 to -6.7
20 to 25	9a	-6.7 to -3.9
25 to 30	9b	-3.9 to -1.1
30 to 35	10a	-1.1 to 1.7
35 to 40	10b	1.7 to 4.4
40 to 45	11a	4.4 to 7.2
45 to 50	11b	7.2 to 10
50 to 55	12a	10 to 12.8
55 to 60	12b	12.8 to 15.6
60 to 65	13a	15.6 to 18.3
65 to 70	13b	18.3 to 21.1

Alaska

Hawaii

Puerto Rico

Mapping by the PRISM Climate Group, Oregon State University, http://prism.oregonstate.edu, 2012

Pollination

Many plants that produce fruits or vegetables also need one more very important thing: help from a pollinator. Pollinators are birds, bees, butterflies, or other insects that spread pollen from one plant to another. The wind can be a pollinator too.

Fruit plants and some vegetables need pollen moved into a certain part of its flowers for each flower to grow into the fruit and vegetables we eat. So if you are growing a plant that will eventually flower and produce a fruit or vegetable, you'll need to place the plant outside where the birds, bees, or other insects can find it and pollinate the flowers.

Tools and Supplies

The list of tools and supplies for many of the projects in this book is pretty basic. A sun-filled window and a jar of water or a garden pot filled with potting soil are often all you'll need to get started. Most of the supplies for the projects are featured in the photograph on page 9. But you should also check the You Will Need list included at the beginning of each project to make sure you have everything before starting to plant. If you have trouble finding any of the supplies, see Where to Find Supplies on page 62.

WHY ORGANIC?

In many of the projects, you'll notice that the materials list calls for organic fruits and vegetables. Why organic? When a food is labeled organic, it means that harmful chemicals or pesticides were not used to grow those fruits or vegetables. Some chemicals used on non-organic plants can prevent seeds or roots from sprouting new growth, so using organic produce is recommended for best results.

Before You Begin

Before you begin a project, carefully read through all the instructions. Read about the tools and supplies needed. Gather the supplies you already have, and make a list of those items you'll need to buy.

Set up a place to work. Projects in this book can be done at a table inside or outside or in a corner of the yard. If you sometimes eat at that table, cover it with newspaper, plastic, or a small tarp.

MASON JARS

PLANTING POTS

WATERING CAN

TROWEL

SCISSORS

SPRAY BOTTLE

NEWSPAPERS

Wear clothes that can get dirty. Old jeans, a long-sleeved T-shirt, socks, and tennis shoes are perfect gardening clothes. If you're working outside, wear a hat and sunscreen. And don't forget your gardening gloves! The gloves are made of leather or heavy cloth and are made to protect your hands from thorns, rocks, or tough plant stems. Look for a pair that fits your hands at your local gardening or hardware store.

Once you have your supplies and your work space prepped, you're all set to dig in!

CHAPTER 1
GROWING UP

Wait! Don't throw that away. Don't even toss it in your compost bin. Did you know that many food scraps can be used to grow new vegetables? It's true. In all three of the projects featured in this chapter, parts of plants that appear to be scraps are actually root ends that can be placed in water and set in a sunny window, where they will sprout new shoots and leaves. So clear some space on the windowsill, gather a few jars and other containers suitable for holding water, and let's get started!

GROW ROMAINE LETTUCE FROM STUBS

Romaine lettuce grows in a tall bunch called a head. When you chop up romaine for a salad, the leaves are cut off the thick base of the root stem. But don't throw away that stub. Try this nifty trick. Save the root stem, and stick it in a dish with a little water instead. In a few days' time, you'll see the beginnings of tiny, new lettuce leaves!

YOU WILL NEED

paring knife and cutting board

3 bunches of organic romaine lettuce, with root stems attached

bowl or loaf pan

spray bottle filled with water

1. With the help of an adult, use a knife and cutting board to carefully cut off the root ends of each lettuce bunch. Make the cut about 1½ inches (4 cm) above the root end.

2. Fill a bowl or loaf pan with about 1 inch (2.5 cm) of water. Place the root ends of each lettuce bunch in the water, with the leaf side facing up. The roots should be soaking in the water but not completely submerged.

3. Clear a space for the lettuces on a wide windowsill, table, or plant stand, preferably in a window that faces south and gets lots of sun.

4. Spray the cut leaf tops with water.

5. Check the lettuces each day to see if tiny leaves have sprouted. Spray tops with water daily, and change the water the roots are sitting in every few days.

6. Within two weeks, you should have fully grown lettuce leaves to harvest for salad. To cut off the new leaves, remove the root stems from the water, place them on a cutting board, and have an adult help you trim the lettuce leaves from the stub. Place the root stems back in the water, mist, and set the bowl or pan back in the sunny window to grow more leaves.

Autumn Salad

Romaine lettuce has a fresh, mild flavor and a satisfying crunch, making it popular for salads.

INGREDIENTS

4 cups romaine lettuce leaves, chopped

1 cup thinly sliced apples

½ cup chopped walnuts or pecans (optional)

2 tablespoons red onion slices

¼ cup feta cheese

3 tablespoons olive oil

2 tablespoons apple cider vinegar

2 teaspoons real maple syrup or honey

1 minced garlic clove

salt and pepper to taste

Tip: Not a salad fan? Romaine lettuce leaves can also be left whole and dipped in a creamy hummus or ranch dip.

Mix romaine leaves with apple slices, walnuts or pecans (optional), onions, and cheese in a medium bowl. In a smaller bowl, combine olive oil, vinegar, syrup or honey, garlic, and salt and pepper to taste. Stir dressing quickly with a fork, drizzle over the salad, and toss it to blend.

START YOUR OWN CELERY PLANT

Celery is a nutritious snack that lends a satisfying crunch to a creamy topping. But next time you snack on ants on a log, don't throw away that stem! Celery can sprout new shoots and leaves from its roots. This plant needs lots of water to grow, so be sure to keep the soil moist.

YOU WILL NEED

1 bunch of organic celery, with root stem attached

paring knife and cutting board

shallow bowl

spray bottle filled with water

6-inch (15 cm) diameter pot with saucer

potting soil

trowel

watering can

1. With the help of an adult, use a knife to carefully cut off the root ends of the celery bunch on a cutting board. Make the cut about 2 inches (5 cm) above where all the stalks come together at the root end.

2. Fill the shallow bowl with about 1 inch (2.5 cm) of water. Place the root end of the celery bunch in the water, with the cut stalk side facing up. The root end should be soaking in the water, but not completely submerged.

3. Set the bowl on a windowsill, table, or plant stand in a sunny window.

4. Spritz the cut stalk tops with water.

5. Check the celery each day to see if shoots have sprouted or roots have grown from the bottom. Spray tops with water daily, and change the water that the roots are sitting in every few days.

6. Within two weeks, you should see several stalks with leafy tops sprouting from the root ball. You may transplant the root into a pot with soil.

7. Working outside or on a work space covered with a plastic tablecloth, use a trowel to scoop potting soil into a pot. Place the saucer underneath.

8. Dig a hole 2 inches (5 cm) deep and wide enough to fit the root ball. Insert the celery top, placing the root side down. Cover the roots with soil, and carefully press the area around the roots to cover them.

9. Set the potted plant in a sunny window, and water very regularly. Check the soil each day to make sure it is moist. If the outdoor temperature won't dip below 40°F (4.4°C), the celery can be placed outside in a sunny spot.

GROWING GREEN ONIONS OR LEEKS

Green onions and leeks are cousins to the common onion. They add key flavors in soup, chili, and much more. And both of these plants are harvested with a tiny root system still attached to the plant, making it easy to regrow your own.

YOU WILL NEED

2 or 3 scraps of green onions or leeks, with at least 2 inches (5 cm) at the bottom left

paring knife

cutting board

short, wide glass or bowl

handful of pebbles or marbles

1. If the plant has more than 2 inches (5 cm) above the roots, have an adult help trim it down to that length on the cutting board.

2. Balance the root ends root side down in the glass or bowl. Add pebbles or marbles to prop and steady the plants, making sure the roots touch the bottom of the glass or bowl and the stems remain upright.

3. Add 1 inch (2.5 cm) of cool water to the bottom of the glass or bowl. It should be enough to soak the roots, but not the stems.

4. Set it in a sunny windowsill to grow. Change the water every other day to prevent the roots from rotting. Within a few days, green sprouts will emerge from the center of the leek or onion. This is the new plant, beginning to grow!

5. When the new inner growth is 4 to 5 inches (about 10 to 13 cm) tall, you may harvest it to use in cooking. Lift the leek or onion from the water, place it on a cutting board, and trim off the new growth at the same spot you cut it earlier. Place the roots back in freshwater to grow again.

trimming green onions

trimming leeks

Potato Leek Soup

Green onions can be finely sliced and used raw to flavor chili, salads, or tacos. Leeks, on the other hand, are usually cooked in soups or other dishes. Here's a quick recipe for potato leek soup, which can be a warming, creamy dish for cool weather. Serve with slices of French bread.

INGREDIENTS

1 cup sliced leek whites and tender greens

2 carrots

2 fist-size potatoes

2 tablespoons olive oil

2 garlic cloves, minced

4 cups vegetable or chicken broth

1 teaspoon salt

½ teaspoon pepper

1 teaspoon thyme

½ cup half-and-half

Have an adult help slice leeks. (If you don't have enough, use store-bought leeks to fill the cup.) Slice carrots and scrubbed potatoes. (No need to peel them if they're washed well.) Heat olive oil in a soup pot over medium heat. Add leeks and garlic. Fry for 5 minutes, or until soft. Add carrots and potatoes, and cook for 7 minutes, stirring often with a wooden spoon. Add broth and bring to a simmer. Cover and cook for 20 minutes, or until the vegetables are soft. Have an adult transfer the soup to a blender and puree it. Pour the soup back into the pot, and add salt, pepper, and thyme. Before serving, stir in half-and-half. Heat through and serve with warm, crusty bread.

CHAPTER 2

PUTTING DOWN ROOTS

Sometimes, when I'm busy weeding or planting in the garden, I accidentally break off the branch of a nearby plant. This used to make me a bit sad, but now I know that many plants will sprout new roots if I put them in a jar of water. This ability of plants to grow new roots is the focus of the projects in this chapter. Just think of the possibilities! One healthy plant can be used to root and start several new plants. What are you waiting for?

SPROUT LEMONGRASS FROM THE STALK

Lemongrass is an herb used to add fresh, lemony flavor to soups, teas, and sauces. It is available in the produce section of many grocery stores. By simply soaking the root end of a lemongrass stalk in a glass jar, you can start your own plant.

YOU WILL NEED

1 small glass jar

1 stalk lemongrass, with root end intact

plastic tablecloth

trowel

potting soil

6-inch (15 cm) pot with saucer

watering can

scissors

1. Fill a small glass jar with water, and set it in a sunny window. Place the flat, root end of the lemongrass stalk in the water.

2. Over the next couple of weeks, keep an eye on the lemongrass. Change the water every few days, and check the root end each time for tiny white roots.

3. When several roots have sprouted and the root end of the grass looks as if it has grown "hair," it's time to plant the grass in a pot.

4. Working outside or at a table indoors that has been covered with a plastic tablecloth, use the trowel to scoop potting soil into the pot. Fill it to within 1 inch (2.5 cm) of the top.

5. Use your index finger to push a hole into the center of the pot that's as deep as your second knuckle. Insert the root end of the lemongrass into the hole you just made, and cover it with soil.

6. With the tips of your fingers, press the soil firmly around the base of the grass stalk. Water the grass well, and set in a sunny window to grow. If temperatures won't dip below 40°F (4.4°C), you can place the pot in a sunny area outside.

7. Eventually, several new stalks will begin to grow from the original stalk you planted. When they reach the height of the original stalk, they should look healthy and strong, and you can harvest one of them to use in a recipe or to start another plant. To harvest, hold the base of the main stalk with one hand and use a scissors to cut off a side stalk with the other hand.

8. Before you cut up the stalk to use or to stick it in a fresh jar of water to regrow, smell the base of the stalk. Freshly cut, it smells like lemons!

Lemongrass Ice Cream

Have you ever made your own ice cream? It's easier than you might think. In this recipe, the lemongrass gives a slight lemony flavor to a classic cold and creamy treat. You'll need an instant-read or candy thermometer to make this recipe.

INGREDIENTS

1½ cups whole milk

¾ cup sugar

3 stalks lemongrass, chopped into 1-inch (2.5 cm) pieces

1 cup heavy cream

1 teaspoon vanilla extract

In a large saucepan, combine milk, sugar, and lemongrass. Warm over medium heat until the mixture reaches 170°F (77°C). Do not allow it to boil. Turn off the burner, cover the pan, and allow to steep for 90 minutes. Use a slotted spoon to remove bits of lemongrass from the mixture. Add heavy cream and vanilla extract to the mixture, and use a whisk to mix well. Have an adult help pour the lemongrass mixture from the pan into a large metal mixing bowl. Cover with plastic wrap, and place it in the freezer for 45 minutes. Remove and use a whisk to mix well. Cover and freeze again for 30 minutes. Repeat, stirring every 30 minutes until ice cream is frozen, or for 2 to 3 hours. Leave it in the freezer for at least another 4 hours before eating to allow the ice cream to firm up.

STARTING HERBS FROM CUTTINGS

Do you have one healthy herb plant? It's easy to grow as many as three other plants from that one! Why would you need three plants instead of one? you ask. The possibilities are endless. Plant them in pots you've decorated, and give them away as gifts. Start your own herb stand outside, and sell them to neighbors passing by. Or grow them in the garden, and you could make pesto or herbal tea throughout the growing season.

YOU WILL NEED

1 healthy herb plant, such as basil, parsley, thyme, rosemary, sage, or lavender

1 to 3 pint-size jars

small scissors

plastic tablecloth

trowel

potting soil

1 to 3 (4-inch, or 10 cm) pots with saucers

watering can

1. Fill the jar (or jars) with water, and set it in a sunny window.

2. Using the scissors, carefully trim off one of the healthy-looking side branches from the main stem of the plant. If the plant has several branches, cut off another in the same way.

3. Place the cut end of the herb in the jar of water. Check to see if any leaves are underwater. If so, pull the cutting from the water, carefully trim off those below-water leaves, and stick the cutting back in the jar.

4. Over the next couple of weeks, keep an eye on the herb cuttings. Change the water every few days, and search the stems of the cuttings for tiny white roots.

5. When several roots have sprouted and the stem looks as if it has grown "hair" 2 inches (5 cm) long, it's time to plant the herb in soil. Working outside or at a table indoors that has been covered with a plastic tablecloth, use the trowel to scoop potting soil into the pot. Fill it to 1 inch (2.5 cm) below the top.

6. Dig a 2-inch (5 cm) deep hole in the center of the pot, and carefully insert the root end of the herb.

7. Cover the roots with soil, and use your fingertips to gently pat down the soil around the stem.

8. Water the plant well, and place it in a sunny window to grow. If the temperature won't dip below 40°F (4.4°C), you can move the plant to a sunny spot outside after a couple of weeks.

STARTING NEW PLANTS FROM TRIMMINGS

Cutting off the branch of a plant and sticking it in water to sprout roots works with more than just herbs. You can try this technique with any soft-stemmed plant that has roots. For instance, if you accidentally break off the branch of a tomato plant while helping in the garden, place the broken end in a jar of water. Within a week, you will see roots begin to sprout. When a good "crop" of roots have grown, plant the branch in a pot. Like the herbs, the branch will develop into its own plant.

Basil-Parsley Pesto

Pesto is a tasty herb sauce that is used on pasta, in soups, or as a dip. It is most commonly made with basil, but it can be made with cilantro or parsley as well.

INGREDIENTS

3 cups fresh basil leaves

½ cup fresh parsley leaves

3 cloves garlic, peeled

⅓ cup grated parmesan cheese

¼ cup chopped pine nuts or walnuts (optional)

½ cup olive oil

juice of one freshly squeezed lemon

½ teaspoon salt

pepper to taste

Tip: To make a dip for veggies, combine with 1 cup plain yogurt or sour cream and 2 tablespoons mayonnaise.

Rinse basil and parsley in a salad spinner, and spin them dry. Then ask an adult to help you grind the garlic in a food processor or blender. Add the basil and parsley, and pulse until the leaves are chopped into very small pieces. Use a rubber spatula to scrape the ground-up leaves down the sides of the container toward the blade. Add parmesan cheese and pine nuts or walnuts (optional). Grind until well blended, again scraping down the sides. Add olive oil and lemon juice. Season with the ½ teaspoon salt and pepper to taste. Grind once more to combine. Serve over your favorite pasta.

PLANT A PINEAPPLE

If you take a close look at a fresh pineapple, you might begin to notice that the spiky green top looks a bit like a common houseplant. Why? Because that's basically what it is! Place the stem at the base of these leaves in water to sprout roots, and you've got your very own pineapple plant. For this project, look for the ripest pineapple you can find, with a top that is somewhat loose. Remember, ripe pineapples have a yellow tint to their rough skin and smell deliciously sweet.

YOU WILL NEED

1 ripe pineapple

paring knife and cutting board

shallow dish, wide enough for the spiky stem

water

potting soil

trowel

6-inch (15 cm) pot with saucer

watering can

plastic tablecloth or newspaper

1. Grasp the spiky top of the pineapple in your hands, and twist it slightly from side to side to loosen it.

2. Ask an adult to help cut the spiky top from the pineapple. On a cutting board, slowly and carefully insert the paring knife into the top of the pineapple, right next to the stem. Use a sawing motion to cut all around the stem. Then pull the spiky top off the pineapple.

3. Set the spiky top on the cutting board, and examine the end that was connected to the fruit. Trim away any of the yellow flesh and rough skin until only the hard core of the stem remains.

4. Set the stem end of the spiky top in a shallow dish filled with ½ to 1 inch (1.3 to 2.5 cm) of water. None of the leaves should be completely underwater.

5. Place the dish in a sunny window. Each day lift the stem end from the water and check for root growth along the outside edge. The roots will be short, thick, and white, and they may take one or two weeks to form. Change the water every two days to prevent bacteria growth.

6. When roots are about 1½ inches (4 cm) long, plant the stem in a pot. Working outside or on a work space covered with a plastic tablecloth or newspaper, use a trowel to scoop potting soil into a pot. Place the saucer underneath.

7. Dig a 2-inch (5 cm) hole in the top of the soil, and insert the spiky top of the pineapple, placing the root side down. Cover the roots with soil, and carefully press the area around the roots to cover them.

8. Set the potted plant in a sunny window and water. Check the soil each day to make sure it is moist. Simply stick your finger into the soil up to your first knuckle. If the soil is dry under the surface, give the plant a drink.

9. Within a few weeks, you will notice new leaves growing from the center of the plant. When temperatures outside remain above 40°F (4.4°C), move the plant outside in a sunny spot to allow pollination to occur. In colder climates, keep the pineapple plant in the pot and bring it back inside to a sunny window during the winter months. With consistent watering and sunlight, the plant will eventually sprout a pineapple from the center. Just stay patient—this can take two to three years.

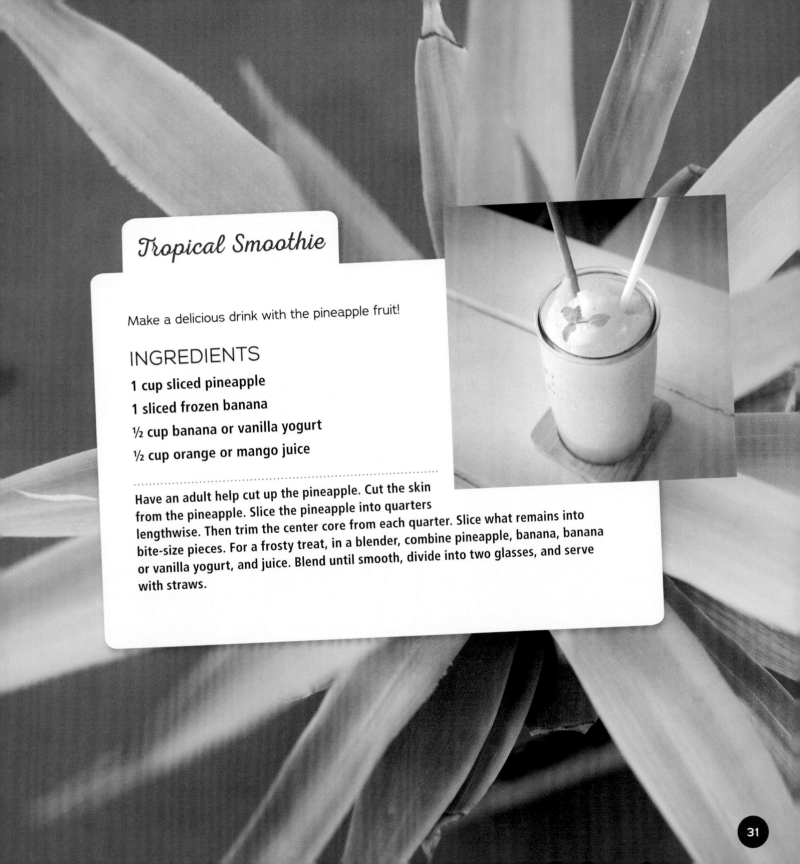

Tropical Smoothie

Make a delicious drink with the pineapple fruit!

INGREDIENTS

1 cup sliced pineapple
1 sliced frozen banana
½ cup banana or vanilla yogurt
½ cup orange or mango juice

Have an adult help cut up the pineapple. Cut the skin from the pineapple. Slice the pineapple into quarters lengthwise. Then trim the center core from each quarter. Slice what remains into bite-size pieces. For a frosty treat, in a blender, combine pineapple, banana, banana or vanilla yogurt, and juice. Blend until smooth, divide into two glasses, and serve with straws.

CHAPTER 3

TUBERS, BULBS, AND RHIZOMES

Tubers? Bulbs? No, those aren't strange vegetables you've never heard of. And you might not even know how to pronounce *rhizomes*, but you're probably familiar with examples of those too. These are all types of plants that grow underground as parts of root systems. They include sweet potatoes (a tuber), garlic (a bulb), and ginger (a rhizome).

We can plant just a part of the root—say, a segment of a sweet potato. When placed in fertile soil, watered regularly, and given plenty of sunlight, that root will multiply and grow a whole new plant. Then the roots of that new plant can be harvested and eaten!

GROW GARLIC FROM A SINGLE CLOVE

Planting garlic is kind of like planting flower bulbs such as tulips, daffodils, or hyacinths in the fall. The amazing thing about planting garlic is that from one head of garlic, you can plant six or more single cloves, or segments, depending on how big the bulb is. Then those cloves will grow into six complete bulbs of garlic over a growing season. How cool is that? If possible, purchase garlic from a local farmer's market or garden store to be sure you are getting a variety that will grow in your area.

YOU WILL NEED

1 or more organic bulbs of garlic, any variety

trowel

6-inch (15 cm) pot with saucer

potting soil

watering can

1. Decide where you'd like to plant the garlic. If you have space for garlic in an outside garden plot, use it! In northern climates where temperatures drop below freezing for part of the year, it's best to plant garlic just before the first hard frost in the fall. If you live in a warmer climate, see "Growing Garlic in the South." Otherwise, garlic can be grown in a pot inside at any time of year.

2. If planting in a pot, use the trowel to fill the pot with potting soil.

3. Use the trowel to dig a hole 3 inches (7.5 cm) deep. If you are planting outside, dig several holes in a row, spacing the garlic 6 to 8 inches (15 to 20 cm) apart.

4. Insert a single garlic clove into each hole with the pointed side up, leaving the papery covering on. Cover each clove with soil, and press the soil down firmly with your fingertips.

5. Use a watering can to water the freshly planted cloves. If you planted the garlic outside, forget about your cloves until spring.

6. Once green shoots poke out of the soil, water and care for the garlic plants as they grow. Soon they'll form scapes—round, curling stems with pointy ends. These are the plant's flowers. When the scapes begin to curl above the rest of the plant, cut them off at the base of the plant, leaving the rest of the green growth standing. Removing the scapes allows the plant to put its energy into growing bigger garlic bulbs rather than producing flowers. (Save the scapes! The stems taste like garlic, and they can be chopped up and added to salads or made into pesto.)

7. When the long garlic leaves turn brown and begin to die off, harvest the garlic. Use a trowel to carefully dig up the bulbs. Cut off the stems. Allow the bulbs to dry for two weeks before using.

GROWING GARLIC IN THE SOUTH

Garlic cloves can be planted outside no matter what zone you are in, but they do best in northern climates. This is because a garlic clove needs to be exposed to temperatures below 50°F (10°C) for six to twelve weeks for the bulbs to grow. If you live where this stretch of cooler weather is uncommon, you will need to "fool" the bulbs into thinking they just endured a winter. To do this, place the cloves in a paper bag, fold it closed, and stick the bag in the refrigerator for ten to twelve weeks before planting.

Certain varieties do grow better in southern climates. Hardneck varieties thrive in cooler climates, but southern gardeners will have better luck planting softneck varieties including Thermadrone, Lorz Italian, Siberian, Bogatyr, Georgian Crystal, and Romanian Red.

Garlic Bread

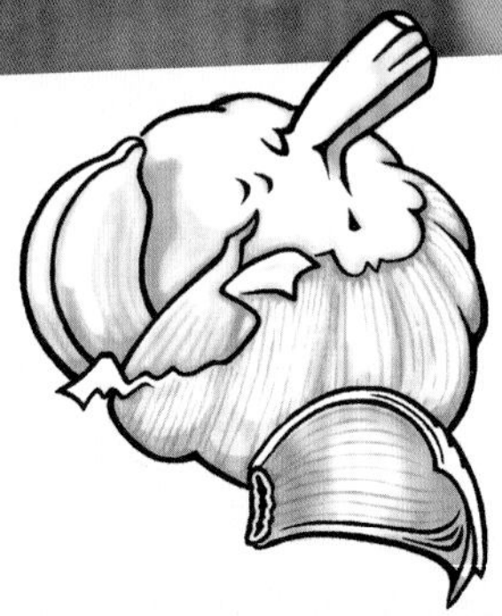

Serve warm garlic bread alongside pasta with pesto for an Italian feast!

INGREDIENTS

1 stick butter, softened

2 garlic cloves, peeled and minced

1 tablespoon fresh parsley, chopped fine

1 loaf French bread

Combine softened butter, minced garlic, and parsley in a medium bowl, and mix well with a fork. Ask an adult to help you slice the French bread down the middle lengthwise. Spread the butter on each sliced side. Place the two buttered halves together, and cut the loaf into 2-inch-wide (5 cm) slices. Wrap the sliced loaf in aluminum foil, and bake at 350°F (177°C) for 15 minutes.

START GINGER FROM A ROOT

When you think of roots, you may think of the thin, white threadlike roots common to most plants. But ginger is a special kind of root called a rhizome.

Rhizomes are thick, starchy root systems that sprout green shoots and leaves that grow aboveground. The roots store energy so the plant can survive colder months. Gingerroot has a fresh, strong, spicy taste, and it's a key flavor in Thai chicken soup, real ginger ale, and chai tea. Here's how to sprout your own ginger plant.

YOU WILL NEED

small jar

2-inch (5 cm) length of fresh, organic gingerroot

trowel

potting soil

shallow, wide pot and saucer

watering can

1. Fill the jar with warm water, and add the piece of gingerroot. Let it soak overnight.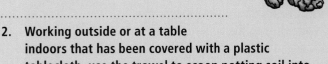

2. Working outside or at a table indoors that has been covered with a plastic tablecloth, use the trowel to scoop potting soil into the pot. Fill it to within 1 inch (2.5 cm) of the top.

3. Dig a hole 2 to 3 inches (5 to 8 cm) deep. Set the gingerroot into the hole with one of the small, nubby bumps sticking up. If your gingerroot has several nubby bumps, consider cutting the root into pieces, each with its own nub, and planting each in a separate pot.

4. Cover the root with soil, and use your fingertips to pat down the soil over the hole. Water it with the watering can. Place the pot near a window (doesn't need full sun).

5. Check the ginger each day, making sure that the soil is moist, and watch for a green sprout. This may take a while, as ginger is a slow grower. (The ginger pictured here took two months to shoot up a sprout. Be patient!)

6. Once a second sprout appears, you can be sure that the rhizomes are branching out. To harvest some of the root for use, use a trowel to carefully dig down along one side of the pot until you reach the rhizome. Uncover a 1 inch (2.5 cm) length of root, and have an adult help you cut the root. Cover the hole again with soil, wash the root, and use it in your favorite recipe.

Homemade Ginger Ale

Ginger—a root with a fresh, spicy flavor—is used to season everything from drinks to soups, meats, sauces, and stews. Homemade ginger ale is a tasty treat that's quite different from commercial brands. Here's how to make your own:

INGREDIENTS

1½ cups peeled, chopped gingerroot

2 cups water

¾ cup sugar

pinch of salt

1 quart (1 L) sparkling water

1 lime, cut into quarters

ice cubes

Combine chopped gingerroot and water in a medium saucepan, and heat on low for 45 minutes. Turn off the heat, cover the pan, and allow the mixture to steep for 20 minutes. Use a sieve or colander lined with cheesecloth to strain the mixture over a bowl to remove pieces of ginger. Press strained ginger against the strainer to remove all the liquid. Pour the strained liquid back into the saucepan, and add sugar and a pinch of salt. Stir and cook over medium heat until sugar is dissolved, forming a syrup. Turn off the heat, and allow the mixture to cool to room temperature. Transfer syrup to a jar or small pitcher, cover, and chill for three hours, or until cold. For each serving, pour ⅛ cup ginger syrup into a glass. Add 1 cup sparkling water, juice squeezed from a quarter of the lime, and ice. Stir and enjoy.

SPROUT A SWEET POTATO

At first, this project may look a little silly sitting on your windowsill, but be patient. Before long, a tangle of roots will sprout from the bottom, purple or green shoots will emerge from the top, and delicate leaves will begin to unfurl.

YOU WILL NEED

1 organic sweet potato (small enough to fit inside your jar)

small and medium-sized jars

scissors

1 gallon (3.8 L) terra-cotta pot with saucer

potting soil

sand

trowel

1. Set the sweet potato in the jar, and fill the jar with water. The sweet potato should rest on the bottom of the jar with the top couple of inches of the sweet potato rising above the top of the jar. Set in a sunny windowsill.

2. Check the sweet potato each day to make sure it has plenty of water, as it may evaporate. If the water looks cloudy, pour it out and refill the jar with freshwater. Otherwise, just let the sweet potato alone.

3. Eventually roots will begin to sprout from the bottom. (This will probably begin within a week.) Then a week or so later, tiny nubs of shoots will become visible on the top of the sweet potato.

4. When the potato has plenty of roots and several shoots, harvest some of the shoots for planting. Use the scissors to carefully snip off a shoot, right where the stem meets the sweet potato. Repeat with two other shoots. Place the broken end of each shoot into a small jar filled with water. Set the jars in a sunny window, and check on them each day. Within about two weeks, they should sprout roots.

5. When the shoots have grown a healthy amount of roots, plant them in a mixture of soil and sand. Use a trowel to fill the pot most of the way with about two-thirds potting soil and one-third sand (available at gardening stores). Stir the mixture with the trowel to combine.

6. Dig three holes in the center of the pot, spaced 2 inches (5 cm) apart and about 2 inches deep.

7. Place a sweet potato shoot into each hole, roots down. Cover with soil, taking care not to damage the shoots or leaves. They should start just below the surface of the soil.

8. Place the pot where it will get sun for part of the day and shade for part of the day, and water it. Keep potted sweet potatoes inside for the first 12 weeks. Then sweet potatoes can be moved outside as long as temperatures remain above 40°F (4.4°C).

9. Water sweet potatoes once a week.

10. Sweet potatoes will be ready to harvest within 150 days. To harvest, use a handheld garden fork to gently turn the soil to find the sweet potatoes.

11. Place harvested sweet potatoes in a cardboard box or paper bag, and set in a warm place for 10 days to cure (dry). Then they are ready to be washed or peeled and cooked!

Sweet Potato Oven Fries

INGREDIENTS

2 large sweet potatoes

⅛ cup olive oil

1 teaspoon salt

¼ teaspoon ground black pepper

½ teaspoon sugar

¼ teaspoon chili powder

ketchup or other dipping sauce

Preheat the oven to 450°F (232°C). Wash the sweet potatoes, pat dry, and then peel off the skin. Cut a sweet potato in half lengthwise, and then cut it into ½-inch-wide (1.3 cm) slices. Repeat with the other half, and then do the same with the second sweet potato. Place the cut fries in a large bowl, and toss with olive oil. In a small plastic container with a lid, combine salt, ground black pepper, sugar, and chili powder. Cover tightly with the lid, and shake well to mix. Next, spread the fries on a cookie sheet and sprinkle evenly with spice mixture. Place the cookie sheet in the oven, and bake for 10 minutes. Remove, use a spatula to flip the fries over, and bake for another 10 minutes. Remove from the oven, and allow to cool slightly. Serve with ketchup or your favorite dipping sauce.

CHAPTER 4

SAVE THOSE SEEDS!

You probably already know a thing or two about growing plants from seeds. Packets of ready-to-plant seeds are available at garden stores, hardware stores, grocery stores, and farmers' markets. Did you know that all of those seeds were gathered from individual fruits, vegetables, or flowers? And did you know you could gather seeds yourself? Collecting your own seeds to plant is easier than you might think!

How is it possible for a tiny seed such as one from a bell pepper to grow into a full-size plant that produces more peppers? Every seed contains the food it needs to sprout into a seedling. When that seed is planted in healthy soil, watered, and placed in a sunny spot, the food within the seed is transformed into the energy needed to grow. First, the seed sends out roots. Then the green seedling sprouts through the top of the soil. Once leaves unfold from the seedling stem, they begin to convert sunlight and water into energy needed to grow.

PEPPER IN A NEWSPAPER POT

Bell peppers may be the easiest seeds to harvest and grow from scratch. Simply cut open a pepper, brush the white seeds from the pepper's inner membrane, and the seeds are ready for planting. Bury the seeds in soil, water, and place in a sunny spot. Before you know it, you'll be the proud grower of a new pepper plant.

When choosing a pepper to start with, remember that seeds from a red, orange, or yellow pepper will grow a plant with peppers of the same color. Seeds from a green pepper, though, will likely grow red peppers, once the peppers are fully ripe.

Wondering what to do with the harvested peppers? They are delicious sliced into strips and dipped in ranch dressing or the basil-parsley pesto on page 27. Or heat a tablespoon of olive oil in a skillet over low heat and fry the pepper slices with slices of onion. Stir every five minutes or so. After about 15 minutes, the peppers should be very soft and the onions should be soft and yellow with slightly browned edges. Add a ½ teaspoon of sugar, and stir to caramelize the onions and peppers. Serve with pasta or as a topping on pizza.

YOU WILL NEED

1 organic bell pepper, any color

paring knife

cutting board

small bowl

plastic tablecloth or newspaper

trowel

potting soil

6 to 8 newspaper pots

waterproof tray to hold pots

spray bottle filled with water

watering can

HARVEST THE SEEDS

1. Ask an adult to help you cut the pepper in half on the cutting board, using a paring knife.

2. Open up the pepper, and tap it on the cutting board, cut side down, to remove the white seeds. Transfer the seeds to a small bowl until you are ready to plant them.

PREPARE THE POTS

1. Make the newspaper seedling pots, following the instructions (see pages 49–50). Six to eight pots should be plenty.

2. Set the newspaper pots right side up in a waterproof tray.

3. Cover your work space with a plastic tablecloth or newspaper. Use the trowel or a kitchen spoon to fill each newspaper seedling pot with potting soil.

PLANT THE SEEDS

1. Use your index finger to poke a hole in the soil, stopping at your first knuckle. Make two more holes.

2. Drop three pepper seeds into each hole.

3. Cover the holes with soil, and carefully pat them down with your fingertips.

4. Spray the soil surface in each pot with water until completely moist.

5. Set the pan of seedling pots in a sunny window to grow. Spritz the soil in each pot with water every day. Seedlings should sprout in 7 to 10 days.

6. Continue to check on the seedlings each day, watering them when the soil is dry to the touch.

TRANSPLANT THE SEEDLINGS

1. When the seedlings are sturdy and about 3 inches (about 8 cm) tall, they're ready to be moved into a 6-inch (15 cm) pot or into the ground. (You don't need to remove them from the newspaper pots—just plant the whole thing!) If planting in a pot, use a trowel to fill it with potting soil, stopping 3 inches (8 cm) from the top.

2. Dig a hole in the center of the pot that is just deep enough to hold the seedling paper pot.

3. Place the paper pot into the hole, cover the top with soil, and use your fingertips to firmly pat the soil around the plant.

4. Water well and place in a sunny spot.

MAKING NEWSPAPER SEEDLING POTS

Here's an easy way to make seedling pots with materials you might otherwise recycle. One double-page spread from most newspapers will make two pots. The newspaper used here is about 12 inches (30 cm) wide by about 22 inches (56 cm) long, but a newspaper of a slightly different size is OK.

YOU WILL NEED

4 sheets of newspaper

1 (14-ounce, or 0.4 kg) can (for example, from canned beans or fruit)

clear tape

1. Unfold a two-page spread of the newspaper on a table in front of you. Carefully rip the page in half, right down the center fold line. You will have two pages, each measuring about 22 inches by 12 inches (56 cm by 30 cm). Set aside the other half for the next pot you make.

2. Fold the sheet in half from top to bottom, and then fold in half again from right to left. Your folded sheet of paper should measure 11 inches by 6 inches (28 cm by 15 cm).

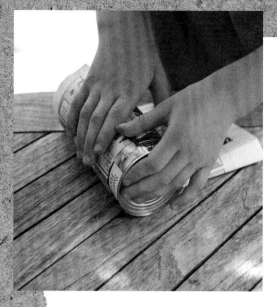

3. Set the folded sheet in front of you with the fold line on the right. Lay the can on its side across the fold, with about 1 inch (2.5 cm) of the can to the right of the folded edge. Place it near you, toward the bottom edge of the newspaper.

4. Lift the bottom of the newspaper to meet the side of the can. Hold it there while you roll the can up to the top of the page.

5. Use two pieces of clear tape to hold the seam.

6. In three or four sections, fold the excess paper on the left side against the bottom of the can and use a couple of pieces of tape to secure it, creating the bottom of your newspaper pot. Place the can right side up, and gently pound the bottom of the can against the tabletop to flatten it.

7. Slide the paper pot off the can. Repeat these steps to make as many pots as you'd like.

YOUR OWN PUMPKIN PATCH

The next time you carve a pumpkin for Halloween, set aside a handful of seeds to plant in the spring. You'll need some space in a garden for this project, as pumpkin vines need room to spread out. A 5-foot (1.5 m) square area should be enough. If you don't have a yard, see if there's a community garden nearby where you might be able to plant your seeds. Be sure to ask one of the gardeners for permission before planting.

YOU WILL NEED

newspapers or a plastic tablecloth

sharp knife

soup spoon or serving spoon

large bowl

colander

dish towel or paper towel

envelope

trowel

6 seedling pots such as newspaper pots (see pages 49–50), or 2 (1-pound, or 0.5 kg) plastic strawberry clamshell containers with lids

potting soil

waterproof tray to hold pots

spray bottle filled with water

watering can

HARVESTING THE SEEDS

1. Set the pumpkin on a work space covered with old newspapers or a plastic tablecloth.

2. Ask an adult to cut the top off the pumpkin. The easiest way to do this is to insert the knife several inches out from the stem and use a sawing motion to cut a circle around the stem.

3. Pull the top off the pumpkin, and set it aside. Use the soup spoon or serving spoon or your hands to scoop the seeds and stringy flesh out of the inside of the pumpkin. Place everything in the large bowl. Once most of the insides are out, use a spoon to scrape the sides of the pumpkin clean.

4. Separate 20 seeds from the slime, and place them in a colander over the kitchen sink. Run cool water over the seeds to rinse them clean. Place the washed seeds on a clean dish towel or paper towel to dry overnight.

5. The next day, place the dried seeds in an envelope and seal it. Label the envelope with "pumpkin seeds" and the date. Place this envelope in a cool, dry place until next spring. (Remember where you've put it!)

PLANTING THE SEEDS

1. If you live where temperatures dip below freezing for part of the year, start seeds indoors three to four weeks before the last frost. (Check your local weather reports for an approximate time frame.) Transplant seedlings outside one week after the danger of frost has passed.

2. Cover your work space with newspaper or plastic tablecloth. Use a trowel to fill six seedling pots or two plastic strawberry containers with potting soil.

3. Use your index finger to poke a hole into the soil, stopping at your first knuckle. Make two more holes if you are using newspaper pots or five more holes if you are using a plastic strawberry container. Place pots or the container on the waterproof tray.

4. Drop three pumpkin seeds into each hole, and cover with soil.

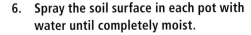

5. Carefully pat down the top of the holes with your fingertips.

6. Spray the soil surface in each pot with water until completely moist.

7. Set the pan of seedling pots in a sunny window to grow. Spritz the soil in each pot with water every day. Seedlings should sprout in 7 to 10 days.

HARDEN OFF SEEDLINGS

When seedlings have grown a few leaves and a sturdy stem, help them transition to life outside. Up until now, the seedlings have had ideal conditions for growing: they've been kept moist, had a consistent growing temperature of around 70°F (21°C), and have not been exposed to wind or heavy rain. If they are to survive the changing weather, they will have to get used to the outside environment—*gradually*. This process is called "hardening off" the seedlings. Here's how to do this:

1. On day 1, place the seedlings in a shady spot outside that's sheltered from the wind for 1 hour.

2. On day 2, place the seedlings in the same place outside for 2 hours.

3. On day 3, place the seedlings in place where they will be exposed to a little more wind and some indirect sunlight. Leave them outside for 3 hours.

4. On each following day, leave the plants outside for one more hour, exposing them to a little more wind and sunlight each time. By the seventh day, the plants will remain outside in full sun for 7 hours. Then they are ready to be planted in the ground or in pots and remain outside for the rest of the growing season.

TRANSPLANT SEEDLINGS

1. When the danger of frost has passed and the plants have been hardened off, sturdy pumpkin seedlings may be planted outside in a sunny garden spot. With the trowel, dig holes in the soil just deep enough to fit the seedling pots. Cover the pot edges with soil, and pat down around the plants with the palms of your hands. If you planted the seedlings in a plastic strawberry container, water the seedlings well to secure the soil, around the roots. Have an adult help you use a trowel to remove the seedlings from the container and place them into the holes. Pat the soil firmly around the seedlings.

2. Use a watering can to water well. Check the soil each day to make sure it is moist.

3. As the vines grow, you may need to "show" them where you'd like them to grow by moving the vines, guiding them through a fence or onto a trellis. A small strip of cloth can be used to tie vines to fences or trellises.

4. Eventually, big yellow flowers will appear on the plant. Allow these flowers to grow—they are the beginnings of the pumpkins. Not all the flowers will produce pumpkins. Pumpkins usually reach full size in 100 to 120 days after the seeds are planted. They will turn from green to orange as they ripen.

Crunchy Pumpkin Seeds

Wondering what to do with the remaining seeds you scooped from the pumpkin? Make them into a crunchy snack!

INGREDIENTS

Seeds from 1 pumpkin

2 tablespoons olive oil

salt and pepper to taste

½ to 1 teaspoon chili powder (optional)

Separate the seeds from the stringy flesh, sorting each into separate bowls. Toss the stringy part into your compost bin, if you have one, or throw it away. Then put the seeds in a colander, rinse under cool water, and drain. Preheat the oven to 350°F (177°C) with one of the oven racks in the center position. Pour the seeds onto a cookie sheet. Drizzle the olive oil on them, and sprinkle salt and pepper to taste and chili powder, if using. Mix oil and seasonings into seeds by turning the seeds over with a spatula. Bake on the center rack in the oven for 15 to 20 minutes, or until lightly golden brown. Allow to cool completely before serving.

LEMON TREE IN A POT

Have you heard the saying, "When life gives you lemons, make lemonade"? Well, with just a single lemon, you could grow your own lemon tree—and *then* make lemonade! Lemon, orange, and grapefruit trees can all be grown using the instructions provided here. Citrus trees such as these take a long time to start producing fruit—usually ten years or more. But meanwhile, these plants are decorative and easy to care for.

YOU WILL NEED

1 organic lemon

cutting board

paring knife

¼ teaspoon measuring spoon

plastic tablecloth

trowel

potting soil

2 (6-inch, or 15 cm) pots with saucers

spray bottle filled with water

watering can

1. Place the lemon on the cutting board, and have an adult help cut the lemon in half.

2. Use the ¼ teaspoon to scoop all the seeds out of both halves of the lemon, and place them on the cutting board. Discard any seeds that have been cut with the knife.

3. Cover your planting work space with a plastic tablecloth.

4. Use the trowel to fill the pot with potting soil. Stop when the soil is 1 inch (2.5 cm) below the rim.

5. Gently push the lemon seeds into the surface of the soil as deep as your first knuckle, keeping a distance of 2 inches (5 cm) between each seed. Plant as many seeds as will fit in the pot.

6. Cover the seeds with soil, and use your fingertips to gently pat down the surface.

7. Use the spray bottle to mist the surface of the soil until it is very moist. Set the pot in a sunny windowsill to grow.

8. Check on your lemon seeds each day, spraying the soil with water. After one to two weeks, you should begin to see tiny green sprouts poking through the top of the soil.

9. Once seedlings have sprouted, you can begin to water with a watering can whenever the soil is dry to the touch.

10. When the seedlings have grown to a sturdy 2 or 3 inches (5 to 8 cm) tall, choose which two look the strongest. Then pull up the other weaker-looking plants. Leave one of the sturdy lemon seedlings in the original pot. Use a trowel to carefully move the other to the other pot, filled with potting soil. Water both pots well. Continue to care for the lemon trees, and they will grow a couple of feet tall. Eventually the tree will produce blossoms that will turn into lemons. When the tree grows too large for the original pot, transplant it into a bigger one.

Homemade Lemonade

Try this recipe with lemons from the store, if you don't want to wait until your tree begins producing fruit!

INGREDIENTS

7 lemons

2 cups cold water

1 cup ice cubes

¼ to ½ cup superfine sugar

Squeeze the juice of 6 lemons into a glass measuring cup. Strain the juice to remove the seeds. Pour lemon juice, water, and ice cubes into a pitcher. Add ¼ to ½ cup superfine sugar, depending on how sweet you want your lemonade. Stir well to combine. Cut the last lemon into ¼-inch (0.6 cm) slices. Pour lemonade into glasses, and serve with a lemon slice.

GLOSSARY

acidic: soil that has a pH measurement of 4.0 to 6.5. Some plants, such as blueberries and strawberries, grow best in acidic soil.

alkaline: soil that has a pH measurement of 7.0 to 7.5. Some plants, such as sunflowers, grow well in alkaline soil.

bulb: a plant, such as garlic or daffodil, that grows from a globelike root underground

climate: the average or typical weather conditions in a region over time

compost: a mixture of decayed food scraps, plants, and soil that is rich in nutrients

flower: the part of a plant where the seed or fruit grows

hardening: getting a seedling used to living outside in sun, rain, and wind

herb: a plant that is used to flavor food

neutral soil: soil with a pH measurement of between 6.0 and 7.0. Some plants, such as pumpkin, lettuce, and many other vegetables, grow best in neutral soil.

organic: plants that have been grown without the use of chemical fertilizers or pesticides

pH: a measure of chemicals that make up soil that affects how easily plants can take in nutrients from the soil

photosynthesis: how the leaves of plants convert sunlight into the energy they need to grow

pollination: the spreading of pollen from one flower to the next

potting soil: a balanced mix of clay, sand, silt, and humus that is ideal for growing healthy plants

rhizome: a plant, such as ginger or iris, with a thick root system that grows underground, storing energy for the plant

seedling: a young plant

transplant: to plant a seedling in a larger pot or in the ground

trellis: a structure, usually made out of wood or metal, that is used to support the branches of a plant

trowel: a small gardening tool with a curved blade that can be used to break up soil and scoop up dirt

tuber: a starchy root, such as potatoes or sweet potatoes, that grows underground and stores energy for the plant

GARDENING RESOURCES

BOOKS

Bartholomew, Mel. *Square Foot Gardening with Kids: Learn Together.* Minneapolis: Cool Springs, 2014.

Cornell, Kari. *The Nitty-Gritty Gardening Book: Fun Projects for All Seasons.* Minneapolis: Millbrook Press, 2015.

Fossen Brown, Renata. *Gardening Science Lab for Kids: 52 Fun Experiments to Learn, Grow, Harvest, Make, Play, and Enjoy Your Garden.* Beverly, MA: Quarry, 2014.

Hendy, Jenny. *Gardening Projects for Kids: Fantastic Ideas for Making Things, Growing Plants and Flowers, and Attracting Wildlife to the Garden, with 60 Practical Projects and 500 Photographs.* London: Southwater, 2012.

Lovejoy, Sharon. *Roots, Shoots, Buckets & Boots: Gardening Together with Children.* New York: Workman, 1999.

Tornio, Stacy. *Project Garden: A Month-by-Month Guide to Planting, Growing, and Enjoying All Your Backyard Has to Offer.* Avon, MA: Adams Media, 2012.

GARDENING WEBSITES

Kid's Gardening
http://www.kidsgardening.org/
Provides resources and ideas for gardening at school and at home. Click on the Kids Garden News tab for gardening activities and tips each month.

My First Garden
http://extension.illinois.edu/firstgarden/
Learn helpful tips for beginning gardeners, such as when to begin planting outside in the spring and what tools to have on hand.

USDA Plant Hardiness Zone Map
http://planthardiness.ars.usda.gov/PHZMWeb/
Use this map to locate your growing zone.

WHERE TO FIND SUPPLIES

Big-Box Stores

Stores such as Target or Walmart carry seeds, pots, and other gardening supplies and tools.

Home Improvement Centers

Most of these stores such as Home Depot, Lowes, or Menards have a garden center where you can find most everything you'll need for the projects in this book.

Local Co-op Grocery Store

Many food co-ops carry organic seeds in the spring. This is also a great place to buy organic sweet potatoes, garlic, lemons, lemongrass, and gingerroot.

Local Farmers' Market

This is a great place to find seeds, seedlings, herbs, and organic vegetables that thrive in your area. Search for your nearest farmers' market on the USDA website http://search.ams.usda.gov/farmersmarkets/Accessible.aspx.

Local Garden Center

You'll find most everything you need at your local gardening center: seedlings, seeds, pots, tools, gardening gloves, compost, and soil.

Local Hardware Store

Look here for seeds, gardening tools, pots, soil, trellises, and more. Some hardware stores may sell seedlings, herbs, and vegetable plants as well.

Online Stores

Online selling sites such as Amazon are an easy, go-to source for general gardening supplies and gardening books.

Seed Savers Exchange

http://www.seedsavers.org/ Seed Savers Exchange is dedicated to preserving a wide variety of heirloom seeds. Look here for unique seeds that you can't find anywhere else.

INDEX

ABOUT THE AUTHOR

Kari Cornell lives to garden, cook, and craft. She is the author of many books for kids, including *The Nitty-Gritty Gardening Book* and a number of titles in the You're the Chef cookbook series and several STEM Trailblazer Bios. Cornell lives in Minneapolis with her husband, two boys, and their crazy dog, EmmyLou. To learn more and read her week-by-week account of the past gardening season, go to karicornell.wordpress.com.

ABOUT THE PHOTOGRAPHER

Jennifer Larson started photographing—and gardening—when she was a kid, and she has done both ever since. She gardens with her own kids, tending a vegetable garden along with cherry, apple, and peach trees. She was the photographer for *The Nitty-Gritty Gardening Book* and has written several children's nonfiction books as well. She lives in Minneapolis with her husband and two kids.